OVERCOMING UNIMAGINABLE PAIN

THE ROCK THAT IS HIGHER THAN I

BY

EVELYN RUTENDO MAKANDA

ISBN: 978-0-620-77252-5

Scripture quotations marked NKJV are taken from New Kings James Version of the Bible. Copyright © 1982 by Thomas Nelson Publishers

Scripture quotations marked KJV are taken from Kings James Version of the Bible, also known as the Authorized Version.

Published by:
Faithland Publishers (Pty) Ltd
234 Malibongwe Drive, Northriding,
Johannesburg, South Africa.
+27 11 702 7876
info@faithlandpublisher.co.za
www.faithlandpublisher.co.za

Cover and layout designed by Twinz Solutionz
www.twinxsolutionz.co.za

This book was printed in South Africa.

To order additional copies of this book contact:
Contact Person: Evelyn Makanda
Email: overcomingunimaginablepain@gmail.com
evelynmakanda@gmail.com

Mobile: +27 73 998 9625

TABLE OF CONTENTS

DEDICATION

To my beloved mum, Rufaro Gredesi Sinzara Lord, you have sacrificed so much and loved me unconditionally. You inspired all that I have become in life today. My late father Richard Biggy Nyamayaro Makanda you will always have a special place in my heart.

To every person hurting, dealing with loss and facing unfathomable pain this book is dedicated to you, you will get through this.

ACKNOWLEDGEMENTS

I would like to thank The Lord God Almighty who gave me the strength and wisdom to write this book. The Holy Spirit inspired and breathed into the inception and completion of this book.

I wish to thank my mother for her support, cheering me on and believing in me when no one else did.

I would like to thank my grandmother Madren Simaunda thank you so much for your love and support, you are a great General.

A special thank you my Elizabeth, my prayer partner, my champion, my shoulder to cry on. Joyce Vongai Mutendi Daramola, you prayed with me in the valley and celebrated with me on the mountain. You are such a blessing to me.

I acknowledge and thank my spiritual parents Pastor Tich and Princisca Tanyanyiwa for believing in me, praying for me and inspiring me, sharpening me and never giving up on me.

To everyone who contributed to the publishing of this book, thank you for your tireless efforts and hard work.

God bless you all.

FOREWORD

Jesus said, I have told you these things, so that in me you may have perfect peace and confidence. In the world, you have tribulation and trials and distress and frustration; but be of good cheer, take courage; be confident, certain, undaunted! For I have overcome the world. I have deprived it of power to harm you and have conquered it for you. This book goes beyond just words but gives the true living words of life when faced with challenges. As you go through these pages you will experience the Ruach, the very breath of God that gives you life.

I have seen the transforming power of God in Evelyn. The book is an outward expression of her testimony of what God has done for her. The morning I received the phone call, of the unimaginable news, my prayer was Lord, show yourself strong. There is no age that is appropriate to go through such storms but you still look and think but Lord she is still so young and she does not deserve it. Indeed no one deserves it because it is the enemy that comes to kill, steal and destroy. The strength of your faith is tested during the times of storms and tribulation. It is very simple to talk about having gone through storms, compared to the process of going through the storms. Jesus said that trials and tribulations are in this world, but! The conjunction but changes the course of what could be. But! you are to step out and decide to be of good cheer. There is a position you take, even through pain and sorrow. No one can make that decision for you. You choose to either wallow yourself in the pain when life comes against you or choose to be a victor. When you choose to wallow yourself in the pain the harvest of that is not healing but you will get yourself into depression. This means you are now facing more than the one initial tribulation, but you simply open yourself to sinking into a deeper hole.

Evelyn will walk with you how not to pay attention to the feelings of what you are going through. She sites, more importantly, the humanity of what Jesus had to face, and that the pain that Jesus went through was for you and me. She brings clarity and understanding how you can attain your victory by leaning on Jesus, the Rock, the One who understands the infirmity of man. When you chose to surrender and worship, when you choose to have deep intimate conversations with God, when you choose to embrace and understand the heartbeat of God for your life, you come out with another testimony like Evelyn. You come out strong, victorious and well able to press into the good plans that God has for you.

This book is a testimony that no storm can change the course of your life and destiny that God has for you. Only be strong and courageous for the Lord loves you!

Pastor Princisca Tanyanyiwa
Senior Pastor: Prevailing Word Ministries International

INTRODUCTION

I thank God for this opportunity to share my story with you. The story you are about to read may induce feelings of pain and sorrow due to the expression of the pain I went through. However, my intention is not for you to be sorrowful, nor for you to feel pity for me. NO! My prayer is that this testimony will add to your faith, causing you to continue to stand on God's promises.

I postponed writing this book for quite some time. When I eventually sat down to write, it was easy; in fact, the book writing experience felt like there was a fire burning in my spirit - I could not contain it.

The Holy Spirit whispered to me that I must have written a book before I turned thirty years of age. Thus, at the time of writing the book, I was four months away from turning thirty years. When I started writing, I had a conviction and assurance from the Holy Spirit that by the time I turned thirty, this book would have been launched. When I sat down to write I did not even know exactly the words I needed to put down but the Holy Spirit instructed me to grab my laptop and to start typing. I had an assurance from the Holy Spirit that I would complete the writing part in less than a week, and that's exactly what happened.

The book writing experience was quite pain-free because when I started writing I could not stop. The Lord was with me. The Lord spoke to me and said, "Evelyn you have a story to tell and you can no longer delay it further." The first scripture that the Lord gave me was from **Exodus 3:12** which says,

> *"So He said, "I will certainly be with you, and this shall be a sign to you that I have sent you".*

In response, I obeyed God's voice and began to write. The Holy Spirit was very instrumental in the writing process. He ministered to me such that in some instances I would literally stop writing to worship God, to thank Him for His faithfulness, His loving kindness.

I believe that as you read this book, the Holy Spirit will minister to you in a mighty way. I went through a difficult time and came out victorious because my faith was anchored in God's hope. If you are currently going through a difficult time, I believe the Lord will see you through too. Hold on to the hope we have in Him. You are God's masterpiece, heaven knows your name and your story. You are the breath of God, the Ruach of God. If you can surrender your pain to Christ half the battle is won. Surround yourself with people you can be vulnerable with your emotions and your pain, people who will embrace you and encourage you in the love of Abba Father.

As the Holy Spirit ministered to me while I was writing this book, I began to realize that God has proven Himself to be faithful over and over again. It brought back so many memories of when the Lord held my hand through it all. Be comforted that no matter what you may be facing today, though you may not see how you will get through today or tomorrow, the Lord promises that He will be with you until the very hand. He says in Matthew 28:20,

"…and lo I am with you always, even to the end of the age'.
Amen.

The story of Shadrach, Meshach and Abednego is a source of encouragement. These men were faced with a difficult situation of being forced to worship a false god that had been set up by King Nebuchadnezzar. The three man had such confidence and faith that their God would save them from the wrath of the King. The Bible says in **Daniel 3:17-18,**

"If that is the case, our God whom we serve is able to deliver
us from the burning fiery furnace, and he will deliver us
from your hand, O King. " But if not let it be known to you,
O king that we do not serve your gods, nor will we worship
the gold image which you have set up".

In the later verses, Shadrach, Meshach and Abednego were thrown

into the fire but were not hurt. Their faith in God caused King Ne
buchadnezzar to bless the name of God and a decree was passed tha
the entire nations should worship their God, **Daniel 3:28**. You ma
not understand what you are going through now but God is settin
you up for success. God had the power and ability to stop Shadrach
Meshach and Abednego from being thrown into the fire but he didn'
He allowed for it to happen but they came out from the other side un
scathed and unharmed. I challenge you today to believe that you to
will come out on the other side unharmed. We serve a powerful God
He is mighty and His hand is upon your life. Hold on to His promise
over your life. Everything you are going through now is working fo
your good.

Of the painful situations I experienced, I had never imagined or ex
pected them to happen to me. Sometimes we hear the painful stories o
other people and we disqualify ourselves from ever experiencing such
pain. I knew that life was generally marked by challenges, but I ha
not expected that I would be a recipient of such painful challenges.
remember my conversations with the Lord and crying out to him an
saying Lord, "I know a lot of much older women who have not eve
faced such challenges but why I am going through this?"
One wise man once told me that if God could show us the entire pic
ture of our life, He would cease to be God. He keeps certain things hid
den from us because He is God. All secrets of the universe are know
to God. He is all knowing and all powerful; nothing you are goin
through today surprises God. He is the Alpha and Omega, the begin

ning and the end. The word of God says in **Jeremiah 1:5**,

"Before I formed you in the womb I knew you"

There is no other scripture that illustrates how intimately God knows each and every one of us. He knew you before you were formed in your mother's womb. Therefore, your entire existence is in His hands. God has never promised us that we will not go through challenges but He promises us that whatever challenge we go through He will be with us. He says *"He will never leave you nor forsake you"* **Deuteronomy 31:6.**

You maybe reading this today and saying Evelyn, you have no idea what I am going through; you may be experiencing unfathomable pain. Yes, I may have no idea what you are facing, what you have lost or what you are about to lose, but one thing I am certain of is God is still on the throne. For as long as He is on the throne, He knows what you are going through. He will never leave you nor forsake you. His promise to us is to help us get through the pain. Each person's grief is unique to them and you will experience it differently.

Two people may have the exact challenge but be guaranteed that their experience will not be the same. During the time I was hurting and going through pain, the Lord gave me a scripture **Psalms 61:2** says,

"From the ends of the earth I call unto you, when my heart is overwhelmed lead me to the rock that is higher than I."

This scripture helped me to walk through some of the most difficult seasons in my life, which I will share in the coming chapters. My heart was so overwhelmed and the pain was so tangible I wished I was able to take it out of my heart, but I remembered there is a rock that is higher than I and that rock is Jesus Christ whom I have come to know as Yeshua Hamashiach ("Jesus Christ" in Hebrew). In my pain and sorrow, I held on to an everlasting hope.

Chapter 1

WHEN UNIMAGINABLE PAIN COMES YOUR WAY

A few years ago I met a gentleman who was everything I ever dreamt of in terms of a life partner. He was kind, caring, handsome, loving, patient; in him were all the good things I had wished and asked God for. In fact, he was just the perfect guy for me and I was so happy and over the moon when we met. I grew to love him and we began to date. The relationship was so sweet, it was the best relationship I have ever had at the time. I enjoyed the relationship and everything was going very well. We both knew from the time we met that we definitely wanted to get married and be together for the rest of our lives.

There was nothing that could have stopped us from being together and eventually getting married. As time went on we began to introduce each other to our friends, family, extended family, church friends and so forth. We travelled to many places together and created the best memories. The love was so good and he was totally dedicated to me. He treated me like a queen with the uttermost respect. It was indeed a dream come true; everything I had hoped for and prayed for in a man had finally come to me and I could not stop thanking God for him. The wishes and plans for my life were finally coming together. I envisaged a happy and long life with him.

Within a year of dating, he took the next step and proposed to me. It was indeed a glorious day, the happiest day of my life. This man I loved dearly asked for my hand in marriage, on my birthday. This was the best birthday gift ever. It was a beautiful warm Saturday in December, the African sun up high in the sky shining so bright. I cried tears of joy as he took out the ring, went down on one knee and asked the magical question. He put the ring on my finger and asked me to be his wife. It was the most gorgeous ring I had ever seen. I knew in my heart that it was meant to be and I said yes! I remember calling my mum, my family and letting everyone know that I was engaged with a grin from ear to ear and a thankful heart to God. I had always wanted to be married before I had turned thirty years of age. Our close friends and family joined us in the celebration, as I still believe some of them knew that he was going to propose.

We started planning for our engagement party and knowing myself it was going to be nothing short of amazing. If I was going to be married once I was going to make sure I would give myself everything I had ever dreamt of and that included a glamorous engagement party and a wedding to die for. The planning was set in motion and I literally went all out in terms of how I wanted the event to look and feel. I was definitely not going to spare any change and deprive myself of any luxuries. It is every woman's dream to get engaged and have the wedding of their dreams thus, I was no exception. The day finally arrived, it was a glorious day, and I had family travel all over to celebrate my engagement party with me. I was nervous and excited - a multitude of emotions were going through me. The day was an incredible success and everything was up to the standard I had imagined being the perfectionist that I am.

Soon after the engagement party, we started looking forward to the lobola (a traditional practice wherein the groom pays the bride's family dowry) wedding day and then the big white wedding. I had all my colors picked out, venue, suppliers everything was already planned because I am a well-organized person. , Due to the fact that I like to plan things in advance, I was going to have nothing short of a perfect wedding.

The following December we travelled to Zimbabwe and did the formal family introductions. I had mentally and emotionally prepared myself to be a wife and I knew that the time had come and nothing could have stopped it from happening. The most powerful tool one can ever possess is intention. I was determined to be a wife and was looking forward to my glorious marriage.

A few weeks before the traditional customary marriage day was due to take place, I had not gone to work and I had just woken up going about the house doing the usual housework. This was a bit odd for me not to go to work. My spirit was unsettled but I did not know why I was just uneasy and my heart was very heavy because my fiancé and I had been in a very bad argument. I kept thinking to myself that maybe it was because of the argument, therefore, I ignored the feeling. An hour after I woke up, I had a visit from two dear friends, a couple that had known my fiancé and I very well. It was very odd that they would be coming to my house at that time of the morning, on a working week day; they also came in separate vehicles. As soon as I opened the door for them my heart sank, I saw the look on their faces as they asked me to sit down. I knew that something terrible had happened. They informed me that my fiancé had been involved in a car accident the previous night and had died on the scene. The man I had loved, the man who had loved me, the man I had planned to wed and be married to for the rest of my life was gone. I could not fathom the situation I was faced with. I could not understand it neither could I register what I was being told. How does this happen? Why does this happen to children of God?

The questions I began to ask myself are typical questions that we ask when we go through painful situations. It's almost as if being a child of God disqualifies us from going through certain things. Are you going through a situation that you cannot handle, is it so painful and you are asking God questions? You may even be thinking that since you were faithful to the Lord why would you be punished this way! This is the perfect time for you to understand that the Lord has not left you. He will never leave you nor forsake you. It may be hard to expect life to continue after such things but just believe it. My mind didn't want to believe what I was hearing but yes, my beloved fiancé had passed away.

I remember the pain was so heavy in my heart; it was almost tangible, if I could remove it from my heart and put it in my hands, I would have but of course, it's not practical. Certain life trials seem so far-fetched until they come knocking on your door. Never in my wildest dreams did I think it would ever happen to me and nothing could have prepared me for it. I was so broken, I was shattered. My whole world came crashing down when the reality sank in. I didn't know what to do or what to say. You may have gone through a similar situation and still holding on to the pain, you may have been molested when you were a child and robbed of your innocence or bullied in school. Whatever situation you have gone through, understand that there is life after the situation – the pain and shame will go away if you allow yourself to see this possibility.

I met a lady who fell in the hands of unscrupulous individuals and lost a lot of money. She thought she was investing in a business venture only to find out the deal never existed. She was so hurt because she had put all her life savings into the non-existent business. A year later God restored all her money when she got a double promotion in her work place. Some people are wrongly convicted and spend decades in prison, someone may have tarnished your reputation; there is a lot of things that may hurt us throughout the journey of life but we are not to give up on life.

A dear friend of mine grew up with people around her who spoke negatively into her life and never had anything positive to say about her. She grew up with a low self-esteem thinking she will amount to nothing. Today, she is a happily married woman running a successful business. This maybe you today, instead of being a victim, God wants you to recover what has been stolen from you. He wants to heal you and restore your joy.

In the book of Genesis, when God looked for Adam and Eve it wasn't because he didn't know where they were, of course, he did. But it was a call to the relationship because we are designed to live in communion with God. The bible is essentially a story of God seeking to restore His relationship with us. God wants you to know that a relationship with Him is a relationship that you can trust. For many years, I put up a facade that everything was okay while I was hurting deeply inside. Many of my relatives never knew why I was so quiet and reserved, as I never talked much or shared much. I build up walls so high no one could ever come in.

I created a world wherein could never trust anyone with my emotions. One day I woke up and I was tired of it all. I gave my heart to Christ and withheld absolutely nothing, I found people I could trust; people I could share my thoughts and emotions with. These were people I could confide in; they embraced me with the love of the Father.

Sometimes all you need is to be embraced with the love of our heavenly Father. Therefore, if you were hiding from the world, take off the mask as you do not have to hide any longer. God knows where you are and who you are.

Many of us have mastered the art of putting up an award winning performance while we are hurting from experiences from our childhood, from a devastating diagnosis, or a broken family. God wants to fill you up with hope and love. He wants to take away the pain. It took me a long time to realise I could come to God with my pain, but it became very important for me I had to take that step to open up to God through a relationship with Christ. God began to take off layers and layers of hurt and replaced them with a renewed sense of identity, love, peace and purpose.

God's arms are always wide open to receive us, it doesn't matter what you might have done or the shame that you may feel. God is love. Never be swallowed by the world and by your shame. There are gifts that God has bestowed upon each and every one of us. Life is meaningless without Christ and His love. We have to come to a place of utter surrender when God lifts you up from that place. With God, you have the assurance that your light will once again shine so bright regardless of what you may have gone through.

My desire is for everyone who is reading this book to understand that going through pain does not relegate you to a life of pain forever. In that journey of recovering your life, so many things will evoke memories around you. You may find it hard to sleep and loneliness will feel like a visitor who has overstayed their welcome. For many months I felt like this.

However, I chose to hold onto God's hope and promises over my life. It was hard, it was painful but I held onto His garment of peace and did not let go. Pain has a way of attracting other similar things like sorrow, regret and depression. I began to miss my father who passed away when I was only fifteen years old. I wished he was alive; I thought it would make it easier for me to go through life's challenges had he been alive.

I began to wish my mother had never left me to go to the United Kingdom in search of greener pastures for us. But I was reminded that there is nothing which happens in life surprises God. He doesn't wake up and say, Oh my, now what do I do things have gone horribly wrong. God has already covered all the bases, He knows what has happened and what will happen. **Ecclesiastes 3:15**, says,

> *"That which is has already been, and what is to be has already been, and God requires an account of what is past".*

God is outside of time. He is the past and the present and the future. He is beyond a timeline. He knows, sees and makes what was, what is and what is to come. May this truth set you free!

Chapter 2

GRIEVING WITH HOPE

Going through each day after I received the fateful news was painful. Seconds went by like hours and hours went by like days. I remember one day I was sitting on my couch and I was having a conversation with God. I was telling Him how painful it was and how much I needed Him to take the pain away. The Lord showed me a vision of a boat that is anchored at harbor. No matter how powerful the storms maybe, the boat would not move. It may be tossed from side to side, it maybe be shaken, waves may rise upon it but because of the anchor, it was held down to its place. The boat would not go anywhere.

The Lord was telling me to anchor in His hope. He was saying to me, Evelyn I am allowing you to grieve, the fire will not consume you, the storms will not drown you, only have hope. I implore you to understand that the storms you are facing right now will one day be over. You may not see the way out right now; it may seem like your whole world has come crumbling down. Find your hope in God, hold on to His promise, that He will never leave you nor forsake you. Hold on, you are a boat that cannot be moved. God has hidden your destiny behind your tears. This process makes you tough and you will come out a diamond. It purges your unbelief and prepares your heart for what God intends to do. God's presence is with you in the process.

The word of God tells us in **1 Thessalonians 4:13** that we ought to grieve with hope. One lesson I learnt during my trying times was that you cannot resist the process of grieving otherwise it will catch up with you later. I am of the view that, you should not allow anyone to not give you the time and space to grieve. There are many examples of men and women of God in the bible who grieved; I will highlight on such cases in the coming chapters. Due to the way God created you, (spirit, soul and body), you will grieve whether you like it or not, you will be hurt at some point. God gave us the soul; the part of our being that allows us to feel emotions. Allow yourself to grieve but remember the hope we have in Christ. After every storm, there will be a calm. Weeping may last for a season but joy comes in the morning, as the bible promises us. Take refuge in the hands of our Father; take comfort under the wings of our Lord Yeshua Hamashiach.

One of the spiritual disciplines I practiced a lot was praying for the peace of God to invade my life. Praying became an important aspect of my life as I was dealing with the loss. I urge you that if you are going through a similar situation or if you ever find yourself in a similar situation you pray for God's peace. Remember the story of Jesus and the disciples in **Mark 4:35-41**. The disciples were on the boat and a very strong storm arose. The disciples were in utter panic and could not understand why Jesus would be sleeping when they were literally about to die. The disciples assumed that because Jesus was sleeping in the storm, He did not care about their lives. I can certainly say I had moments when I felt like Lord why are you sleeping in the midst of such a great storm? It is very important as children of God to be careful of what we say when we are going through difficult situations. Our words must always be full of hope and they must bring life. The word of God says in **Proverbs 18:21**,

"Death and life are in the power of the tongue".

When Jesus woke up, He silenced the storm and there was a great calm, it was as if they were not about to die a few moments before that. The situation you are facing right now may seem like only death is the way out, it is therefore key to remember that it's not over until God says it's over. God will take the pain away. Allow Jesus Christ the Prince of Peace to visit your storm and silence it.

There is a day where I had a vision as I was praying and asking God to take the pain away. I remember this vision vividly. I saw a man who appeared to me dressed in white and looked so clean; he was calm and so peaceful. The man touched my shoulders gently; from that moment on I knew that the Lord had not left me. He was with me through the storm. I began to have a joy that was unspeakable, a peace I could not explain. When people who knew what I had been through saw me they could not believe it, people would say to me all the time how do you manage to be so joyful after what you went through. I would just smile and say, "The joy of the Lord is my strength". I declare the same to you, may His joy be your strength. **Psalms 23:4** says,

"Your rod and staff, they comfort me."

He is a strong, loving and protective shepherd in whom we can trust.

When I was praying, I understood that I was hurting and I was grieving. I needed to make sure that the spirit of grief does get hold of me. There is a difference between grieving with hope and being consumed with the spirit of grief. The spirit of grief is from the devil and is not of God. Once it gets hold of you, it can steal your joy and cause you to lose the good fight of faith; it will bring to you its friends or accomplices like depression and in many other cases suicidal thoughts. Whatever you may be going through pray against the spirit of grief. The Bible clearly tells us that we must grieve with hope. In **Isaiah 61:3,** the word of God says,

"To console those who mourn in Zion, to give them beauty for ashes, the oil of joy for mourning, the garment of praise for the spirit of heaviness; that they maybe called trees of righteousness, the planting of the Lord, that he may be glorified."

Christ provides comfort to all those who mourn. He will take you out of your horrible situation and give you beauty.

I was told a story of a young lady who had gone through a similar situation that I had gone through. As the story goes her fiancé passed away as they were travelling to her parents' house for their traditional wedding including five other people that were in the vehicle with him. You can only imagine the devastating and unimaginable pain she must have gone through. The day of celebration had turned into a day of mourning. She could not comprehend and deal with the grief to a point whereby the spirit of grief attacked her, she distanced herself from people. She began to drink excessively as alcohol became her escape from the pain she was going through. Nothing and no one could console her; for many years she became a completely different person.

During my season of pain and sorrow, I also learnt of a young lady whose husband died on the day of their honeymoon trip, he was a trainee pilot and as part of their celebrations, he had planned to fly her new bride over the Inyangani mountains in the beautiful mountainous region of Manicaland in Zimbabwe. He had a technical failure with the chopper he was flying and never made it to pick her up. She became a widow on the same day that she was married. Unimaginable pain!

I thank God that my life was preserved from the spirit of grief. God could not have allowed for my life to be wasted. Whatever circumstances you are going through today take comfort in that someone has gone through similar or even worse circumstances but they came out victorious. You are an overcomer. You have the power to stop your life from being wasted. You have to declare that you will get through whatever you are going through. If you can wake up every day and speak those words to yourself, the Lord God Almighty will see you through.

H. Norman Wright in his book, **'Grieving the loss of a loved one"**, states that grief is neither noble nor heroic, it's hard work, it's painful; It's a slow moving process. God's Word will strengthen you and give you a renewed hope for the future,

"For I know the plans I have for you," declares the Lord,
"plans to prosper you and not harm you, plans to give
you hope and future" **Jeremiah 29:11.**

Chapter 3

THE ROCK THAT IS HIGHER THAN I

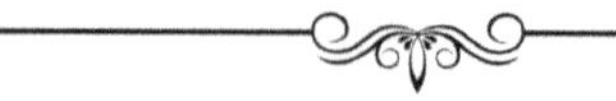

Psalms 61:2, *"From the end of the earth I will cry to you, When my heart is overwhelmed; Lead me to the rock that I Higher than I".*

As I was writing this book and the Holy Spirit instructed me to include this scripture. I didn't see how I could dedicate an entire chapter to one scripture. While writing this chapter, it became evident to me that the Lord wanted me to have this scripture in this book, as it has become one of my personal favorite scripture. My biggest lesson from this scripture is that there is safety in Christ the rock and none in ourselves. I love to just spend time with the Lord alone in my private space, and this space happens to be in my house because that is where I have conversations with God. In these moments, I jump, cry, I laugh, scream and pour out my heart to Him. I lose all dignity and allow myself to soak in His presence, these are moments of sheer vulnerability to Abba Father.

Pain, chaos and turmoil often make it difficult to find the will of the Father. Sometimes we would rather prefer if God dropped His entire plan for our lives right in front of us, but rarely does He do that. But He does say in **Psalms 37:23;**

"The steps of a good man are ordered by the Lord, and he delights in his way"

God will guide you step by step, as long as you believe that He has a future and a plan for you that is perfect according to His will. When Abraham was about to sacrifice his only son Isaac, we can only imagine what was going through his mind. It must have been so hard lifting up that knife, but because it was the will of God, he had to do it regardless and in that moment God stepped in and gave him the next step for his life. You may feel like you have lost so much, you have been robbed so much, believe that God will give you the next step for your life. He has a plan for every season of your life.

In **Matthew 26:36,** Jesus wrestled with the will of God facing the prospects of the reality of the cross. It says in **Matthew 26:37-38** says,

"He began to be sorrowful and deeply distressed. Then He said to them "My Soul is exceedingly sorrowful, even to death."

Jesus Christ was in great agony and anguish. There was a level of incomprehensibility he felt over the impending reality of experiencing the Father's will. Scientists tell us that Jesus Christ experienced a condition called hematohidrosis in which a human being sweats blood. This typically occurs under conditions of extreme physical or emotional stress, essentially chronic stress. Jesus Christ suffered acute stress, fear and mental contemplation of the events that were just about to befall him.

The experiences of the Garden of Gethsemane are so emotional for Him. This was a place of pressing, a kind of pressing and crushing that brings out the anointing. We see the pressure intensifying for Jesus Christ. The Garden of Gethsemane is a place where we see the desires of the flesh wrestle with the will of God. Sometimes the Christian walk is not easy, at times you sweat it out, though it's nothing compared to what Jesus Christ went through for us. Jesus Christ too was afraid in the Garden of Gethsemane, He made the prayer in **Matthew 26:39,**

> *"O My Father, if it is possible, let this cup pass from me."*

This is the apex of Jesus' life of sorrow and grief. The sorrow was so severe that it came close to killing him. It is far greater than any previous encounters He had ever had. To make matters worse, Jesus Christ went to the disciples and found them sleeping. The disciples had been warned by Jesus Christ that they ought to pray lest they fall into temptation **Mark 14:38**. The importance of prayer is expressed in this account to prepare us for triumph when we face challenges. The disciples ended up learning from the disaster of their prayerlessness. It seems we can never prepare enough for challenges but certainly, prayer equips us and strengthens us as it allows God to deploy angels to our aid.

When you are going through the most difficult time in your life, it may seem as though life is going on just fine for everyone else: you may assume that it's a bed of roses. When people are in pain, they often want the entire world to stop and sympathise with their sorrow. People seem insensitive when they are taking holidays and sleeping peacefully at night. A person in pain may not understand how other people are so happy, how people cannot see that they are hurting, or that they are going through agonising pain?.

In the Garden of Gethsemane, the place of pressing, the spirit of God won. The flesh was defeated and by the time Jesus Christ went to the cross the battle had already been won. By the time Jesus walked out of the garden, He knew that He was going to be crucified. The internal battle had between won. The struggle wasn't the physical aspect of nailing Him, but the internal factor which resulted in the spirit having victory. This shows us that we are constantly fighting battles. You may not be fighting one now but we know they are such seasons; when that season comes for you to fight a battle you must be mentally prepared for it. The one thing we learn from Jesus' experience is that when every area of your life is pressed, the spirit must win. You must conquer. The confusing thing for many people is that this battle is not in the physical realm, it's a different kind of battle - one that everyone cannot see because it is internal. The internal struggle does not need an external healing but an internal touch from heaven.

Furthermore, another thing that stands out for me in this text is the role of angels. The Bible says as Jesus prayed, an angel came and strengthened Him and ministered to Him. It is of paramount importance to pray through whatever storm you may be facing as your prayer allows angels to be deployed to your aid. We have many examples of people who prayed in the bible and angels came to help them. Daniel is an example, he prayed before he was thrown into the lion's den and an angel came **Daniel 6:10**.

The Garden of Gethsemane is one of those moments we see the humanity of Jesus Christ, where he is vulnerable and wrestling with the reality of the cross coming later that day. Many times we want a painless Christian walk. Jesus Christ the savior, had to experience pain. In the book of **Isaiah 53:3**, The prophet told us that Jesus Christ would be a man of sorrows and acquainted with grief. He was absolutely not immune to pain as He experienced, what man will experience like rebellion, sickness, rejection, suffering, loss and death. Our Lord saw it all and felt it all. It was literally sorrow upon sorrow, grief upon grief because He not only experienced it but saw what was in the hearts of man. Glory to God that His death provided a way out for us; though we may go through pain, we find comfort in Him knowing that victory is certain.

It is often said that you cannot have the crown without the cup, that the greater the trial, the greater the trust. When I was broken and hurting, I didn't know why God was trusting me so much. But He was leading me to this day when I will be an author. I am so grateful that I prayed earnestly for His will to be revealed to me. I trusted God to give me the next step of my life. As such, I pray that God will give you the next step of your life. You have to have an uneasiness in your heart, that Lord let your will be done. It is not an easy thing to pray for or ask for, yet it is very necessary and you will have to be steadfast. Generally, our lives are about the destination, therefore you cannot reach a destination without taking the journey. You have to obey His will. It's who you are becoming that is important. If you told me five years ago that I would write a book, I would not have believed it. I allowed myself to be in His will. I actually prayed and declared that I was willing. When you do that you evoke the power of heaven and the will of God is the greatest, safest and best place to be.

Chapter 4

GOD'S PROMISES OVER YOUR LIFE

2 Corinthians 1:20 *"For all the promises of God, in him are yes and in him Amen, to the glory of God through us.*

The truly amazing aspect of God's love is that it does not depend on our own "goodness", He loves us for absolutely no reason. His nature is love. I John 4:8 we read that "God is love". He is intentional about His love towards us and His love is unconditional. God is the same yesterday, today and forever; God's unchanging character is expressed in one of His many promises to us in **Numbers 23:19** which states that,

"God is not a man, that he should lie, nor a son of man, that he should repent. Has He said, and will he not do? Or has he spoken and will he not make it good?"

You may have been robbed of your time, money, substance, worth and dignity. Maybe your friends and family deserted you. There are many unforeseen challenges that we may encounter in the journey of life; some are of our own doing while some are completely inflicted upon us by other people.

When my fiancé passed away I was blamed for his death. You can imagine, I was in pain, not fully understanding what had happened to me, and yet some people seemed insensitive to my sorrow. It is generally accepted the truth that everyone has lost someone they dearly loved, it could be a brother, a father, a sister or a child. People may seem to not care about your grief because they are focusing on their grief. It may even add insult to injury and in some cases, relationships may be severed beyond repair when there is an assumption that people are insensitive to your sorrow. We thank God that the Lord teaches us to forgive those who persecute us.

I could go on about the pain I went through, however, the objective of this book is to testify that the Lord is good to us all and faithful to His Word. God has proved throughout history that He keeps His word. When Joshua was coming to the end of his life, he said to the people of Israel,

> *"Behold, this day I am going the way of all the earth. And you know in all your hearts and in all your souls that not one thing has failed of all the good things which the Lord your God spoke concerning you. All have come to pass for you; not one word of them has failed"* **Joshua 23:14.**

Whenever you find yourself in doubt, may the Lord help you remember the good things He has already done for you. A reflection on His promises will prove to you that even in this difficult situation, a solution is always forthcoming. You will notice that God is always aware of your situation. He is aware of your financial situation, He is aware of your marriage falling apart, He is aware of your wayward children. Hold on to his promises over your life and He will surely return you to the place of peace, abundance, joy and overflow. If He has not done it yet, keep fighting the good fight of faith. This is the Lord we serve!

Chapter 5

YOU WILL GET THROUGH THIS!

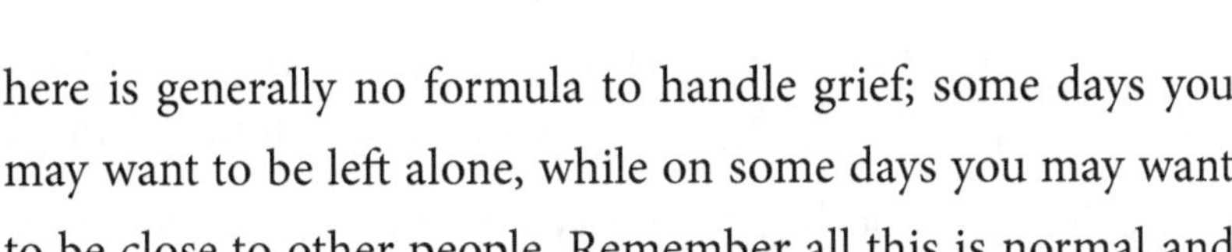

There is generally no formula to handle grief; some days you may want to be left alone, while on some days you may want to be close to other people. Remember all this is normal and you will experience it at any given time or day. I personally believe that the only time you are allowed to be selfish is when you are grieving because the focus at this point is on yourself and no one else.

Allow yourself to be in a position that allows you to heal and for the Holy Spirit to minister to you. You will need to communicate with others effectively so they can know what you want and how they can assist you. Be connected in a good bible based church with believers that will pray with you and stand with you during trying times. Ultimately you cannot do it alone. It will take effort on your part but remember God is with you all the way.

In the case of a losing a loved one, you may have had a daily schedule that was in sync with the person that has passed on. You will need to develop new patterns, take up new hobbies in order to stop the cycle of pain. Do what it takes for you to allow the healing power of God to flow in your life. I enjoy the open air and therefore I took up horse riding. When I would go to the ranch, I would be at peace, in the open fields with the horses, riding and feeding them. I took several solo trips on my own which I can still do until today. It worked for me as my soul would be at peace in the quietness and I could have conversations with the Holy Spirit.

Taking up new hobbies will help to feel in the void caused by losing someone. Before you know it, your time will be occupied with other activities and you begin to form new patterns. Part of the season of grieving is relearning your world. This is not to suggest that you must work towards erasing the memory of that person, you can treasure and create a legacy for them without prolonging the process of grieving. Grieving is for a season, thus it must pass. If it becomes permanent it is now a spirit that can be very dangerous and harmful to you and derail your God given destiny. God gives you a new identity in the world. The Lord God will renew your hopes, desires and dreams and expectations out of your current reality.

One fundamental emotion that I experienced when my fiancé passed away was guilt. If only we had not fought, if only I had seen him the previous day, if only this and if only that. I had so many survivor guilt moments. I felt helpless, frustrated, hurt, angry. So many 'if only' thoughts came into my mind. You may be feeling like you could have prevented the passing on of someone or prevented a robbery from taking place if you had not forgotten to lock the door, if only you had done something differently or if only the events of that day had not gone in a certain way. Some people become so angry at themselves that they live their entire lives in the bondage of survivor guilt; this only prolongs the grieving process. It took me a while to reach a place where I understood that there was absolutely nothing I could have done. **James 4:14** tells us that,

"whereas you do not know what will happen tomorrow,"

No one knows what the future holds. **James 4:15** says,

"Instead you ought to say If the Lord wills, we shall live and do this or that."

In many instances, we are faced with fear. Many people I have spoken to after they lose a spouse is that their future is abruptly changed. You obviously had plans together because you believed this person would be with you forever. Your financial well-being may have been linked to the person who has passed on. But the Bible tells us in **2 Timothy 1:7,**

"For God has not given us a spirit of fear, but of power and of love and of a sound mind."

If you are faced with fear today remember God will always take care of His children. He will provide for every single area of your life. Do not be afraid, when Jesus Christ died on the cross He conquered death. **I Corinthians 15:58** states that,

"Therefore, my beloved brethren, be steadfast, immovable, always abounding in the work of the Lord, knowing that your labor is not in vain in the Lord".

May **Romans 8:35-39** be a reality in your life;

"Who shall separate us from the love of Christ? Shall tribulation, or distress, or persecution, or famine, or nakedness or peril, or sword?"

God's love for his children is infinite. You are God's beloved child. No situation can erase that fact.

I have learnt over time that asking God "why" this and "why" that has happened is the wrong question. When faced with difficult and perplexing circumstances a far better approach is to ask the Lord what he intends to accomplish in your life as a result of the situation.

Chapter 6

GOD'S SUPERNATURAL HEALING AND DELIVERANCE

God uses His servants and His word to bring about deliverance and healing in our lives. As you read through this book, I pray that your spirit submits to the healing power of Jesus. For a long time, I battled with a lot of transgressions that were not pleasing in God's eyes. Because of the fast paced society, we are living in, it is very easy to justify many of our actions as acceptable. The opportunity to sin is all around us, through friends, television, social media and the internet. God's word will never bend to our fleshly desires, He is God, the same yesterday, today and tomorrow, **Malachi 3:6** says,

"For I am the Lord I change not".

For many years I was a born again Christian, spirit filled and still walked in rebellion in a number of areas. God not only wants you born again but free to live your God given destiny. Many Christian leave Egypt only to live forty years in the wilderness and never experience the promised land. When God sets you free completely and you trust His word, you will begin to walk in complete freedom.

What is so interesting is that many of the things I did that were not pleasing to God I didn't see anything wrong with them; little did I know that I was preventing the full manifestation of God's power and grace over my life. It took God's grace for me to realise a lot is at stake and I needed to come back to a place of aligning with His will. When God delivers us, He separates us from all pain, sorrow and curses. I pray that as God delivered me from pain, may it be permanently the same for you.

Apostle Paul assured the Corinthians that,

"No temptation has seized you except what is common to man",
I Corinthians 10:13.

God is so faithful He will not let you be tempted beyond what you can handle, He will also provide a solution and a way out so that you succeed. The church is full of Christians who have secret problems, who are bound with addictions, bitterness, anger, drug abuse, sexual immorality, jealousy, malice. Healing and deliverance is a process that is under God's sovereign control. It is never about the person being delivered but God's supernatural power to set us free. Apostle Paul in **2 Corinthians 1:9-10** writes that,

"But we had the sentence of death in ourselves, that we should not trust in ourselves but in God who raises the dead,

who delivered us, in whom we trust that he will still deliver us".

Without properly acknowledging God as the restorer of your life, there will always be the possibility of failure. I had to thoroughly examine myself to see that I was up for the challenge of God's supernatural healing by acknowledging that certain things were out of line in my life. I did an audit of my heart and life and made a conscious decision and come to a place where I can receive God's supernatural healing. So many prophecies by Pastors and Apostles had been spoken over my life and many had not even begun to manifest. It was only by His power that His spirit located me to deliver me and day after day I begin to see God's power in my life.

Jesus placed great emphasis on the place of Holy Spirit in the life of a believer. He told the disciples that it was better for Him to leave so that they might receive the Holy Spirit **John 16:7**. I am so grateful for God's miraculous deliverance and healing. I pray that it locates you to heal you, to set you free and to deliver you. God's wisdom is a mystery and is beneficial to us, it is through him that we will experience deliverance. **1 Corinthians 2:10** says,

"...For the spirit searches all things, the deep things of God".

Through the word of God, we overcome evil by proving the enemy's

temptations to be lies. Satan is the father of lies as mentioned in **John 8:44**. Deliverance is significant in the process of healing and in closing doors to further attacks by the enemy. The agents of the Kingdom of darkness are not concerned by taking credit in who will get you first rather they are concerned about achieving the mandate to destroy you. The devil will use the challenges we go through to derail our destiny. If we do not take a decisive stance in our walk with Christ, we may not experience total healing. The light of our heavenly Father will shine in every dark area. Do not allow God's healing power to pass you by, you have to be radical and prepare your heart to receive His healing touch. Our God is big and our sins are small.

To partake of God's grace, you need to have an encounter with the giver of grace. The biggest misconception one can ever have is to think that God wants something from us. He has the whole world in His hands. He wants nothing but to love you wholeheartedly. We can not outrun the love of God. He is our everlasting Father, therefore, as we go to our earthly Fathers, we ought to go before expect and receive His healing and unconditional love. Never discount or disqualify yourself from receiving God's love. You are a vessel of God's glory and there is something to achieve through him.

I remember praying and asking God that his cleansing blood and fire would purify me, I reached a point where I didn't care to be undignified. I wanted to be free; I wanted a new lease in life. I acknowledged my transgression, opened up wholeheartedly and his spirit located me. He then began to deal with each and every stronghold that was confining me. God begins to bring you to a place where He restores everything that the devil has stolen from you including your peace and joy. God's deliverance is the supernatural transference of God's people from a place of oppression to a place of freedom. **2 Corinthians 3:4** says,

"For the weapons of our warfare are not carnal, but mighty through God to the pulling down of strongholds".

Like the children of Israel, sometimes we can get so caught up in our place of sorrow that we can not imagine things any better. We can't even begin to imagine the triumph God has for us on the other side of the trial. I didn't want my past to destroy me, neither did I want to be a victim. The amazing thing is we have a wonderful assurance from our Father even in that time when our hearts are breaking. **Psalms 34:18** says,

"The Lord is nigh unto them that are of a broken heart; and saveth such as be of a contrite spirit".

Supernatural deliverance has brought joy to my heart and I have come to understand that it is much more than just winning battles. It is when God reaches down to separate us and supernaturally cut cords of oppression. Deliverance in itself is a miracle. There is a promised land that God has prepared for each and every one of us and the journey to the promised land begins with God delivering us. We have to walk the journey to get there.

The supernatural encounter of God's deliverance cannot be taken lightly; when I started experiencing it, the devil had tried everything in his power to prevent me from this encounter. I had every good reason not to be where I needed to be. When God delivers us, He heals us and it's important to close doors to further attacks by staying as far away from sin as possible and to heighten our sensitivity to the Holy Spirit. By so doing, your life will be restored. **Psalm 14:7** states that,

"Oh, that the salvation of Israel would come out of Zion!
When the LORD restores His captive people, Jacob will
rejoice, Israel will be glad".

God's love is so real and so tangible. This book is not to accept that I have arrived but it acknowledges that I am still on my journey of asking God to teach me how to love Him more with everything in me, how to sacrifice for His kingdom. Even though you are at a point where you felt unloved or unwanted, God will visit your situation only if you fully trust Him. God is the giver of life and since He created your life, you must trust that there is a definite purpose for your existence. Just know that you are at the center of His amazing puzzle. You are God's beloved, His arms are wide open waiting for you to come home.

I pray that this book has assisted you to understand that there is nothing too hard for the Lord. Though the pain may seem indescribable to you, God has already made a way out of such situations. All you have to do is to trust in Him totally, and to understand that you can let go of the pain and accept that He will order your steps out of the dark, into the light!

Prayer

YOU WILL GET THROUGH THIS PRAYER..

Dear Heavenly Father, I am hurting, I am broken, and I am in pain. It is not easy. I ask that you send your ministering angels to comfort me and walk with me during this difficult time. I may not see the way out right now, but help me to anchor in your hope. Lord Jesus, I pray against the spirit of grief and any other opportunistic spirits that may want to materialize on my sorrow. I confess and acknowledge my sins and I, therefore, renounce any soul-tie that is in my life that has been made through sin. Cleanse me with your blood and purify me. Cover me with your peace. Help me to trust in You and to hold on to hope, as long as You are on the throne, I declare that this too shall pass.
In Jesus Name I pray!

Amen!

ABOUT THE AUTHOR

Evelyn Rutendo Makanda is the first daughter of Rufaro Sinzara and the late Richard Nyamayaro. Evelyn Makanda has a Social Science Degree from the University of Witwatersrand Johannesburg, South Africa and International Education from Bard College in New York.

She is passionate about leadership and has several leadership and certifications to her name. Evelyn Makanda is passionate about encouraging young women to live their lives to the fullest and enjoying their season of being single and becoming the best version of what God has created them to be. Evelyn has dedicated herself through her own experience of losing her fiancé just a few weeks prior to their wedding to encourage other people going through similar situations and hurting. From the premise that, we have hope in Yeshua and that the solution is in anchoring in His hope and holding on to His promises over our lives.

Miss Makanda was born in Zimbabwe and is an avid traveller. She currently lives in Johannesburg where she works in Corporate Management and spends her time attending seminars and mentoring other young women.